ODD ADAPTATIONS

WHY DO WOLF SPIDERS MAKE BURROWS?

AND OTHER ODD ARACHNID ADAPTATIONS

BY MEGHAN SHARIF

Gareth Stevens
PUBLISHING

Please visit our website, www.garethstevens.com. For a free color catalog of all our high-quality books, call toll free 1-800-542-2595 or fax 1-877-542-2596.

Library of Congress Cataloging-in-Publication Data

Names: Sharif, Meghan, author.
Title: Why do wolf spiders make burrows? : and other odd arachnid adaptations / Meghan Sharif.
Description: New York : Gareth Stevens Publishing, [2019] | Series: Odd adaptations | Includes index.
Identifiers: LCCN 2018001887| ISBN 9781538220351 (library bound) | ISBN 9781538220375 (paperback) | ISBN 9781538220382 (6 pack)
Subjects: LCSH: Wolf spiders–Adaptation–Juvenile literature. | Arachnida–Adaptation–Juvenile literature. | Adaptation (Biology)–Juvenile literature.
Classification: LCC QL458.42.L9 S53 2019 | DDC 595.4/4–dc23
LC record available at https://lccn.loc.gov/2018001887

First Edition

Published in 2019 by
Gareth Stevens Publishing
111 East 14th Street, Suite 349
New York, NY 10003

Copyright © 2019 Gareth Stevens Publishing

Designer: Sarah Liddell
Editor: Therese Shea

Photo credits: Cover, p. 1 Auscape/Contributor/Universal Images Group/Getty Images; background used throughout Captblack76/Shutterstock.com; p. 4 Artem Orlyanskiy/Shutterstock.com; p. 5 (scorpion) Roman Gilmanov/Shutterstock.com; p. 5 (daddy longlegs) SIMON SHIM/Shutterstock.com; pp. 6, 19 Aleksey Stemmer/Shutterstock.com; p. 7 Katarina Christenson/Shutterstock.com; p. 8 SARIN KUNTHONG/Shutterstock.com; p. 9 Jay Ondreicka/Shutterstock.com; p. 10 KDS4444/Wikimedia Commons; p. 11 Steve Collender/Shutterstock.com; p. 12 McCarthy's PhotoWorks/Shutterstock.com; p. 13 YoThin Pimpanat/Shutterstock.com; p. 14 thatmacroguy/Shutterstock.com; p. 15 Stephen Dalton/Minden Pictures/Getty Images; p. 16 Audrey Snider-Bell/Shutterstock.com; p. 17 Cathy Keifer/Shutterstock.com; p. 18 Sarah2/Shutterstock.com; p. 20 PK289/Shutterstock.com; p. 21 IZZ HAZEL/Shutterstock.com; p. 22 Henrik Larsson/Shutterstock.com; p. 23 frenky362/Shutterstock.com; p. 24 Dutourdumonde Photography/Shutterstock.com; p. 25 (orb web) Norma Stamp at Sunny Daze/Shutterstock.com; p. 25 (spiny orb weaver) Dennis van de Water/Shutterstock.com; p. 25 (funnel web) Koelen/Shutterstock.com; p. 25 (funnel web spider) Amith Nag/Shutterstock.com; p. 25 (tangled web) Juhku/Shutterstock.com; p. 25 (triangulate cobweb spider) FerencSpeder84/Shutterstock.com; p. 25 (sheet web) IanRedding/Shutterstock.com; pp. 25 (sheet web spider), 27 Matauw/Shutterstock.com; p. 28 reptiles4all/Shutterstock.com; p. 29 Tristan Savatier/Moment Open/Getty Images.

Printed in the United States of America

CPSIA compliance information: Batch #CS18GS: For further information contact Gareth Stevens, New York, New York at 1-800-542-2595.

CONTENTS

Words in the glossary appear in **bold** type the first time they are used in the text.

Can you imagine trying to walk around on eight legs? If you can walk like that, you're probably an arachnid! All arachnids have eight legs. Unlike insects, which have six legs, arachnids don't have wings or antennae. Spiders and scorpions are well-known arachnids. Most arachnids have a body made up of two main segments, or parts. Daddy longlegs, mites, and ticks are arachnids that have just one, though.

ARACHNIDS CAN BE AS BIG AS YOUR HAND OR SO SMALL THAT YOU CAN'T EVEN SEE THEM WITHOUT A MICROSCOPE. They've adapted to live all over the world. In fact, there are many living in your home right now!

TICK

4

NO BONES

SPIDERS AND OTHER ARACHNIDS DON'T HAVE BONES. Instead, they have an exoskeleton that keeps them safe. This is called a structural adaptation because it has to do with its body. An exoskeleton is a hard outer shell that protects the arachnid, but lets it move—almost like a suit of armor!

ARACHNIDS HAVE PRETTY STRANGE-LOOKING BODIES, BUT THEY HAVE EVEN ODDER ADAPTATIONS. READ ON TO LEARN MORE!

SCORPION

DADDY LONGLEGS

ALL ABOUT VENOM

SPIDERS AND SCORPIONS ARE ARACHNIDS THAT MAKE VENOM. When a spider catches a tasty insect, the spider bites it and **injects** venom. The venom **paralyzes** the bug. It can't move or escape, so the spider can wrap the bug up in its silk. Most spider venoms are only dangerous to the **arthropods** that spiders eat. Just a handful of spiders in the world have venom that can hurt humans.

Scorpions deliver venom with the stinger on the back of their body. The venom is powerful enough to kill their prey. However, only about 25 of more than 1,200 species of scorpions have venom toxic enough to kill humans.

VENOMOUS OR POISONOUS?

Venomous creatures bite, sting, or stab to do harm, while poisonous animals must be touched or eaten to pass on their fatal effects. The difference is who is doing the action. When spiders bite or scorpions sting, they kill their prey. That means spiders and scorpions are venomous, not poisonous.

THIS IS A CLOSE-UP OF A SPIDER'S MOUTHPARTS CALLED THE CHELICERAE (KUH-LIHS-UH-REE). THEY END IN CURVED FANGS THAT A SPIDER USES TO INJECT ITS VENOM.

7

Color is another structural adaptation arachnids have **evolved** over time. Some spiders, such as the black widow, use bright colors to warn predators away. The black widow spider hangs upside down in its web so other creatures can see the bright red hourglass shape on its abdomen, or stomach. Animals—and people—know to stay away from this dangerous spider because of this shape!

The black widow is one of the few spiders with venom dangerous to humans. The venom can cause pain, stomachache, and trouble breathing. It can even be deadly. **THE VENOM EASILY TURNS BUGS' INSIDES TO GOO SO THE BLACK WIDOW CAN DRINK IT!**

ANT MIMIC SPIDER

ANT MIMIC SPIDER

Ants aren't arachnids, but ant mimic spiders are! **THEY LOOK LIKE ANTS, BUT THEIR EIGHT LEGS GIVE THEM AWAY.** Ant mimic spiders live near ants and blend in with them. They sometimes even copy how the ants act. This is called a behavioral adaptation. They do this so that animals that avoid ants avoid them, too.

IN THE UNITED STATES, BLACK WIDOW SPIDERS ARE FOUND IN DRY, DARK PLACES IN THE SOUTH AND WEST.

Not all arachnids use colors to show they're dangerous. Scorpions are usually colored like their surroundings: brown, yellow, or black. Some spiders are, too.

Brown recluse spiders live in the south and central United States. This arachnid is all brown and has no stripes or bright colors. Its only marking is a brown violin shape behind its head. **THIS SPIDER IS DULL ONLY IN COLOR. ITS BITE CAN BE DANGEROUS TO HUMANS. ITS VENOM CAN DESTROY THE WALLS OF BLOOD VESSELS!** While a bite from a brown recluse can pack quite a punch, this arachnid is very shy. It's rare for it to bother people.

LOOK AT ME!

Peacock spiders are a kind of jumping spider. They use their bright colors to attract a mate. When a male peacock spider sees a female, he sticks his back end in the air so she can see all the colors. **HE "DANCES," SHAKING HIS ABDOMEN AND TAPPING HIS FRONT LEGS.**

PEACOCK SPIDER

PARTS OF A SPIDER

ABDOMEN
CONTAINS SEVERAL
ORGANS

SPINNERETS
SPIN SILK
INTO THREADS

EYES
MOST SPIDERS
HAVE EIGHT

LEGS
ALL SPIDERS
HAVE EIGHT

PEDIPALPS
ARMLIKE LIMBS TO
HELP MOVE PREY

CHELICERAE
MOUTHPARTS,
ENDING IN FANGS

CEPHALOTHORAX
FUSED HEAD AND THORAX,
OR MIDDLE SECTION

A FEMALE BROWN RECLUSE
SPIDER CAN HAVE 150 OR MORE
SPIDERLINGS, OR BABIES, IN A
YEAR. AMAZINGLY, SHE NEEDS TO
MATE ONLY ONCE TO PRODUCE EGGS
THROUGHOUT HER WHOLE LIFE!

EGGS AND BABIES

Not all arachnids mate and have babies in the same way. **SOME FEMALE MITES CAN REPRODUCE WITHOUT MATING AT ALL!** However, most mites mate and lay eggs. When mite larvae hatch, they have six legs. They grow two more legs when they become adults. Ticks reproduce similarly.

Almost all mother spiders lay eggs and create an egg sac wrapped with silk. An egg sac may contain hundreds of eggs. Some mothers leave their sacs. Others guard or carry them around. If a female wolf spider loses her sac, she'll search for it. **SHE MAY PICK UP A STONE AND ATTACH IT TO HERSELF IF SHE CAN'T FIND THE SAC!**

WOLF SPIDER WITH EGG SAC

THIS MOTHER SCORPION WILL CARRY THESE BABIES ON HER BACK UNTIL THEIR EXOSKELETONS ARE STRONG ENOUGH TO PROTECT THEM.

LOVING MOTHERS

Scorpions don't lay eggs like spiders do. INSTEAD, A MOTHER SCORPION HOLDS HER EGGS INSIDE HER BODY UNTIL THEY HATCH. She then carries the babies around on her back until they're big enough to survive on their own. This behavioral adaptation keeps the next generation safe from predators.

GROWING AND MOLTING

Young arachnids grow by molting, or taking off their old exoskeletons. Before molting, they look for a guarded spot so they won't be attacked. Most spiders and some mites make a cocoon to protect their soft bodies while they're molting. **SPIDERS PUMP THEIR BLOOD AND STRETCH THEIR MUSCLES UNTIL THE OLD EXOSKELETON CRACKS!** Underneath is a larger exoskeleton that expands and then hardens.

For many arachnids, the first molt happens while the baby arachnid is still in the egg. **LARGER ARACHNIDS MAY MOLT UP TO 10 TIMES BEFORE THEY'RE ADULTS.**

SPIDERLING

YOUNG TRAVELERS

After orb weaver spiderlings hatch, they "fly away" using a practice called ballooning. Instead of all staying in one place and competing for the same prey, each lets a line of its silk into the wind, which lifts it into the air. **SOME SPIDERLINGS FLOAT MILES AWAY!** Wherever a spiderling lands, it builds its web and begins its life.

MOST SPIDERS THAT SPIN WEBS MOLT WHILE HANGING FROM A LINE OF SILK. YOU CAN SEE THIS SPIDER'S OLD EXOSKELETON ABOVE IT.

15

LET'S GRAB LUNCH

Most arachnids kill and eat smaller arthropods. However, ticks and mites eat liquids from living animals or plants.

Arachnids don't have jaws. How do they eat? **INSTEAD OF TAKING A BITE OUT OF A TASTY BUG, THEY USE JUICES FROM THEIR BODY TO DIGEST THEIR PREY—BEFORE THEY EAT.** Prey may be torn into bits as liquids are thrown up on it, or an arachnid may make a hole in the prey's body and inject liquids. **THEN, THE ARACHNID WAITS FOR THE BODY TO BREAK DOWN INTO A SOUPLIKE LUNCH!** It sucks up the liquefied remains. Arachnids might do this several times until only an exoskeleton is left.

PEDIPALPS

THE MANY PURPOSES OF PEDIPALPS

Like spiders, scorpions have pedipalps. However, scorpion pedipalps have evolved to be much larger. They end in pincers, or claws. Scorpions use these powerful limbs to grab, hold, and tear apart prey. They also can use them to fight enemies, mate, and dig underground to hide from the sun.

DADDY LONGLEGS AREN'T SPIDERS, BUT THEY'RE ARACHNIDS. THEY MAY BE THE ONLY ARACHNIDS THAT CAN EAT PIECES OF PREY THAT AREN'T LIQUEFIED FIRST.

17

There are more than 800 species of arachnids called ticks. Similar to male spiders, male ticks spend most of their time looking for a mate, while females spend more time feeding. A male hard tick attaches to a host—another animal—and drinks its blood. Then he'll quickly drop off and look for a mate.

FEMALE HARD TICKS ATTACH TO A HOST AND DRINK BLOOD FOR AS LONG AS A WEEK, BECOMING ENGORGED. She grows greatly in size and even changes color. Then she mates and drops off the host to lay her eggs in the grass below. Drinking all that blood gives her enough nutrients to have healthy young.

ENGORGED TICK

FEMALE TICKS ARE GENERALLY BIGGER THAN MALE TICKS, AND THEY BECOME MUCH BIGGER AFTER EATING. THESE PHOTOS SHOW A FEMALE TICK BEFORE AND AFTER SHE BECOMES ENGORGED WITH BLOOD.

GLOWING SCORPIONS

All scorpions have a weird adaptation. **THEY GLOW UNDER ULTRAVIOLET LIGHT!** Scientists aren't sure why, but some think it's so that scorpions can see better at night, which is when they're most active. The glow might help them find each other—or perhaps spy and catch their dinner!

ASTONISHING SILK

Silk is some of the most interesting matter on the planet. Spiders aren't the only arachnids that make it, but they have perfected it. Did you know that spider silk is stronger than steel of the same weight?

Spider silk is made in a spider's body and then spun into thread in its spinnerets. The silk is made up of **proteins** similar to those in your hair and fingernails. Spiders use their silk for their homes, hunting tools, transportation, baby care, and more. Some spiders have evolved to make different kinds of silk for different purposes. **ORB WEAVERS MAKE AT LEAST SEVEN KINDS OF SILK!**

IF YOU LOOK CLOSELY, YOU CAN SEE THIS SPIDER'S HAIRY LEGS.

GOOD VIBRATIONS

A spider can tell what's landed in its web—and not by looking with its eyes. Though some have eight eyes, web-building spiders don't have good eyesight. INSTEAD, THEY HAVE **SENSITIVE** HAIRS ON THEIR LEGS THAT HELP THEM RECOGNIZE THINGS IN THEIR WEB. They can tell the difference between prey and another spider walking along their web!

The yellow garden spider is also known as the writing spider because of the way it builds its web. **IT CREATES A ZIGZAG LINE IN THE CENTER OF ITS WEB CALLED A STABILIMENTUM.**

Scientists disagree about why the spider does this. Some say this behavior helps make the web stronger and more stable, while others think the bright white color helps attract bugs for the spider to eat. A few have suggested the spider draws these thick lines to keep birds from flying through and destroying its web, saving it the trouble of rebuilding it. Other kinds of spiders create stabilimenta, too.

WOLF SPIDERS MAKE BURROWS

Wolf spiders don't make webs to catch prey. They're hunting spiders. **THEY HAVE ADAPTED TO DIG A BURROW, OR DEN, AND USE THEIR SILK TO LINE IT.** Then they hide in it and wait for a bug to walk by. When it does, the wolf spider springs from its burrow and catches its prey, dragging the creature into its burrow to eat.

HERE YOU CAN SEE A YELLOW GARDEN SPIDER'S WEB, COMPLETE WITH THE WHITE ZIGZAG STABILIMENTUM.

23

You know most spiders use their silk to make webs, but did you know there are different kinds of webs? Web-weaving spiders are often grouped by the type of web they weave. **IN FACT, SOME KINDS OF SPIDERS CAN ONLY BE IDENTIFIED BY THE KIND OF WEB THEY BUILD!**

SNACKING ON SPIDERWEBS

Some orb weaver spiders use webs only during the day and others only at night. They take down their web each day and then rebuild it. **TO HAVE ENOUGH ENERGY TO DO THIS, IT'S COMMON FOR THESE SPIDERS TO EAT THEIR WEB AS THEY CLEAN IT UP.** They're natural recyclers!

ORB WEAVER

WHICH WEB?

ORB WEB

ORB WEBS ARE ROUND LIKE A WHEEL AND ARE OFTEN FOUND SUSPENDED BETWEEN TWO BUSHES OR TREES OR IN THE CORNER OF A WINDOW FRAME. AN EXAMPLE OF AN ORB WEAVER SPIDER IS A SPINY ORB WEAVER.

FUNNEL WEB

FUNNEL WEBS LOOK LIKE A BIG SHEET WITH A FUNNEL IN THE CENTER. THE FUNNEL IS NOT ONLY A WAY TO TRAP PREY, BUT ALSO A PLACE FOR THE SPIDER TO HIDE. AN EXAMPLE OF A FUNNEL WEAVER IS A BARN FUNNEL WEAVER, WHICH IS FOUND ACROSS THE UNITED STATES.

TANGLED WEB

A TANGLED WEB OR COBWEB IS A MESSY COLLECTION OF LINES OF SILK. THESE WEBS ARE OFTEN FOUND IN BASEMENTS, CLUTTERED AREAS, OR IN PILES OF WOOD OR STONE. BLACK WIDOW SPIDERS MAKE TANGLED WEBS, BUT A MORE COMMON COBWEB SPIDER IS THE TRIANGULATE COBWEB SPIDER, WHICH IS HARMLESS TO HUMANS.

SHEET WEB

A SHEET WEB LOOKS LIKE A BIG BLANKET OF SILK COVERING BUSHES OR GRASS. SMALL, DARK, SHINY SHEETWEB SPIDERS HANG UPSIDE DOWN UNDER THE SHEET WAITING FOR PREY. MANY SPECIES LIVE IN AUSTRALIA AND NEW ZEALAND.

GIRLS AGAINST BOYS

Many arachnid species exhibit sexual dimorphism (dy-MORH-fih-zehm). This means that males and females of the same species look different from one another. **OFTEN, THE MALES ARE MUCH SMALLER AND HAVE DIFFERENT MARKINGS AND COLORS THAN THE FEMALES.** They can almost look like different species!

The reason for this adaptation has to do with making more arachnids. Male and female arachnid bodies are specially adapted to mate and reproduce. **FOR EXAMPLE, FEMALE ORB WEAVER SPIDERS ARE AT LEAST TWICE THE SIZE OF MALES.** Larger females are healthier and better at reproducing. Smaller male orb weavers more easily travel through the wind to find and mate with females.

BAD DATE

SOME FEMALE SPIDERS AND SCORPIONS EAT THEIR MATES. This might seem like a terrible behavioral adaptation, but there's a reason for this! A female needs a lot of **nutrients** to lay eggs that will hatch into healthy babies. Eating the father helps her make certain the young will live.

26

THIS FEMALE GARDEN SPIDER WRAPPED UP HER MATE TO EAT LATER.

One of the largest arachnids in the world is a tarantula. The Goliath birdeater spider grows to be nearly 1 foot (30 cm) from the tip of one leg to another. It's well known for what it likes to eat—anything smaller than it is! That includes frogs, mice, lizards, cockroaches, and even birds.

Still, this big spider is on the menu for snakes and mammals that live in its South American rain forest home. **IT HAS A COOL ADAPTATION TO HELP IT SURVIVE: THE GOLIATH BIRDEATER CAN SHOOT SHARP HAIRS AT ATTACKERS.** The more you learn about odd arachnid adaptations, the more amazing these creatures seem!

28

GOLIATH
BIRDEATER

ARACHNIDS ON YOUR FACE?

How small are the smallest arachnids? **YOU HAVE HUNDREDS OF ARACHNIDS LIVING ON YOUR FACE RIGHT NOW!** Scientists believe all humans have demodex mites living in their facial **pores**. These microscopic creatures are completely harmless and have adapted to survive on either dead skin cells or oil on people's faces.

THE GOLIATH BIRDEATER IS THE HEAVIEST SPIDER IN THE WORLD, BUT THE GIANT HUNTSMAN SPIDER (ABOVE) IS ACTUALLY A BIT LONGER.

GLOSSARY

arthropod: an animal that lacks a backbone and has a skeleton on the outside of its body, such as an insect, spider, shrimp, or crab

digest: to break down food into a form the body can use

engorged: swollen and completely filled with liquid

evolve: to change or develop slowly, often into a better or more advanced state

inject: to force a liquid into something

microscope: a tool used for producing a much larger view of very small objects so that they can be seen clearly

nutrient: matter that plants, animals, and people need to live and grow

paralyze: to make something lose the ability to move

pore: a very small opening on the surface of your skin that liquid comes out through when you sweat

protein: a necessary element found in all living things

sensitive: able to sense very small changes in something

ultraviolet: used to describe rays of light that cannot be seen and that are slightly shorter than the rays of violet light

venom: poison that is produced by an animal and used to kill or injure another animal, usually through biting or stinging

FOR MORE INFORMATION

BOOKS

Dell, Pamela. *Arachnids.* North Mankato, MN: Capstone Press, 2017.

Franchino, Vicky. *Scorpions.* New York, NY: Children's Press, 2015.

Marsh, Laura. *Spiders.* Washington, DC: National Geographic Children's Books, 2011.

WEBSITES

Kidzone Spider Facts
www.kidzone.ws/lw/spiders/facts.htm
This site has a lot of fun facts about spiders.

Scorpions
kids.nationalgeographic.com/animals/scorpion/
Find out more about scorpions.

Spiders for Kids
mrnussbaum.com/spiders-for-kids/
Learn about many different kinds of spiders here.

INDEX